ISBN No 978-1-84535-460-2

The first sight of the famous red and black stripes.

Dennis the Menace arrived in The Beano comic in March 1951. Drawn by artist David Law, the first strip was a black and white half page and Dennis wore a plain grey shirt and striped tie. This changed to a black and white striped jersey within six weeks and then in September, to his now iconic red and black hooped top, probably the most recognisable uniform in British comics. The addition of a mischievous grin and wild, unruly hair completed the style that had to live up to the billing 'The World's Wildest Boy' and in doing so created the first 'punk' look.

Dennis broke the mould (and that wouldn't be all he'd break) from previous comic stories. He was the first anti-authority rebel to (dis)grace the pages of The Beano and The Dandy. His sole quest was to have as much fun as possible and pompous figures of authority and killjoy parents weren't going to stop him. The wilder the mischief Dennis got up to, the more the Beano readers loved him. Teachers and school authority were top targets for the spiky haired terror, creating a battleground that would be in action for decades.

There was no stopping the red and black striped menace and he soon took over the coveted full colour back page of The Beano . Dennis was on a roll and then chanced upon a stray Abyssinnian Wire-haired Tripehound in August, 1968. Impressed by the hound's granite-shattering teeth, Dennis called his new pal Gnasher. Like Ant and Dec or Morecambe and Wise, Dennis and Gnasher became a great comic duo. They elbowed Biffo the Bear from the front cover of The Beano and shortly after launched their own fan club - by 1988 it had a million members. Nothing stopped the terrible twosome and they went on to a puppet series then animated videos before landing their own animation TV series. In this, Dennis's 60th birthday year, the third series is on BBC TV and topping the ratings. Many things have changed in Dennis the Menace's 60 years. One thing has never changed - HE'S STILL THE WORLD'S WILDEST BOY!

Dennis's "steam-roller" fairly makes folk holler.

DENNIS the MENACE

DENNIS the MENACE

DENNIS the MENACE

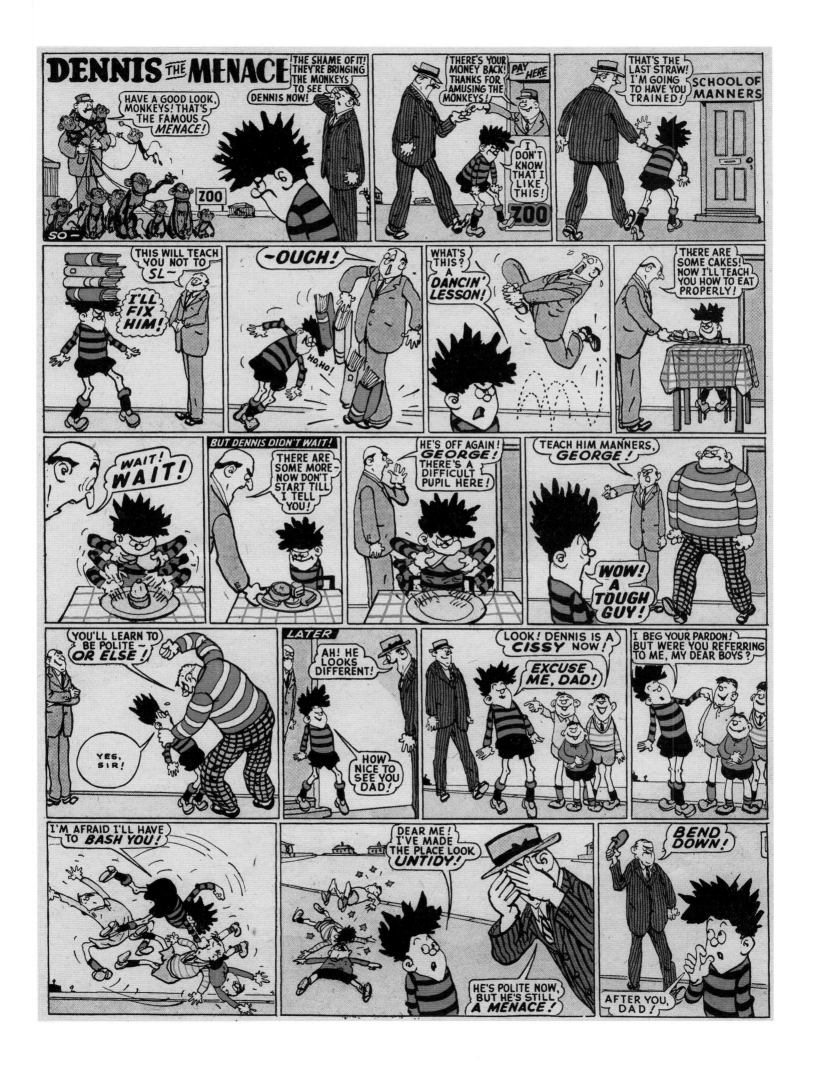

DENNIS the MENACE

DENNIS the MENACE

DENNIS the MENACE

DENNIS the MENACE

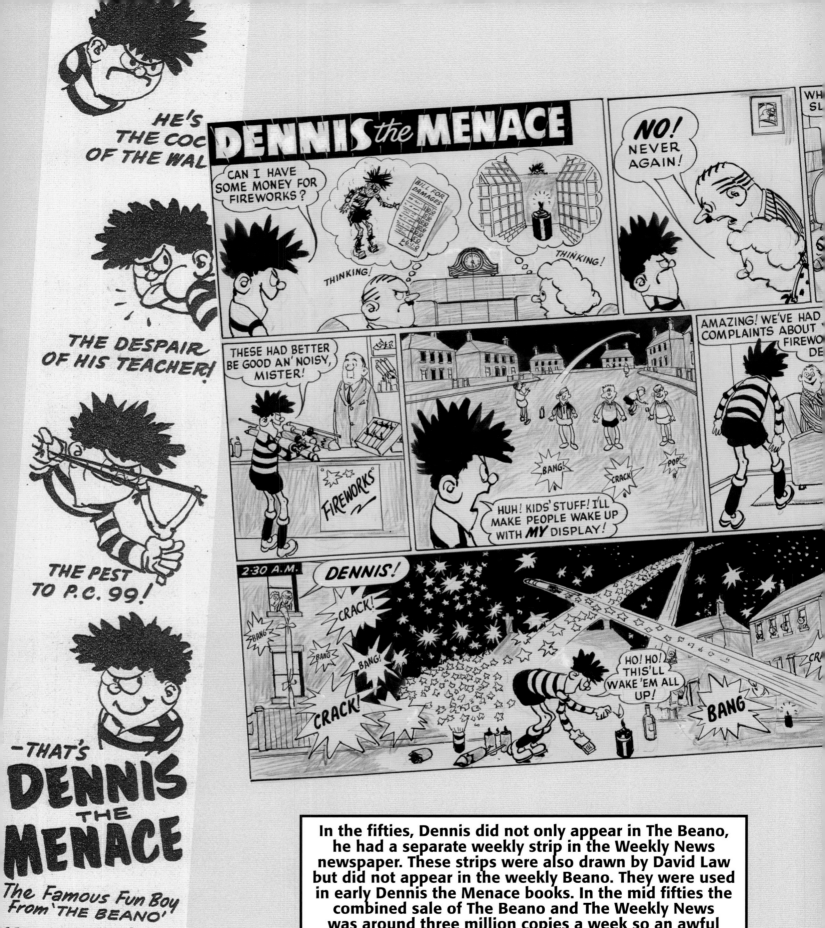

Cover of the Dennis the Menace book 1956.

Dennis the Menace book 1958.

DENNIS'S MODEL CAREER

Robert Harrop Designs started producing figurines based on the characters from The Beano and The Dandy comics back in 1994. Here he tells of his design work with Dennis the Menace. The First Dennis the Menace was sculpted by Matt Buckley in August 1994. The Dennis we chose was one drawn by David Sutherland in 1970. With Dennis the obvious lead character we launched an initial range of 12 Figurines in 1995. The collection was a great success and there was an immediate call for a Christmas piece for the Following year. In conjunction with The Beano we held a competition for the readers to create a Dennis and Gnasher Christmas design. Thousands of entries were received, the youngest entrant was 5 and the oldest 63. The winner was 9 year old Mark Simms from Hull and our studio worked faithfully from his winning sketch and so Santa's Little Helpers became the first Beano Christmas Figurine. This was so popular that it has since become a much anticipated tradition.

Over the last 15 years Dennis the Menace has featured in over 57 models, depicting the work of several different Beano artists. Two of the most notable pieces were the 2001 Red Nose Dennis, sold in conjunction with Comic Relief and the Lost Wax Bronze of Dennis 50th anniversary figure. This was a limited edition of 20 and literally sold out in minutes. We are currently producing the Six Ages of Dennis to celebrate his 60th anniversary, starting with the unique collar and striped tie drawings by the original artist David Law. This was superseded in just weeks by the iconic red and black hooped jersey we all know and love. For your interest we have included photographs of the sculpting, casting and painting of the first 60th anniversary figure.

Sculpting

Casting

Fettling

For further information about
The Beano and Dandy figurines
visit www.robertharrop.com

Painting

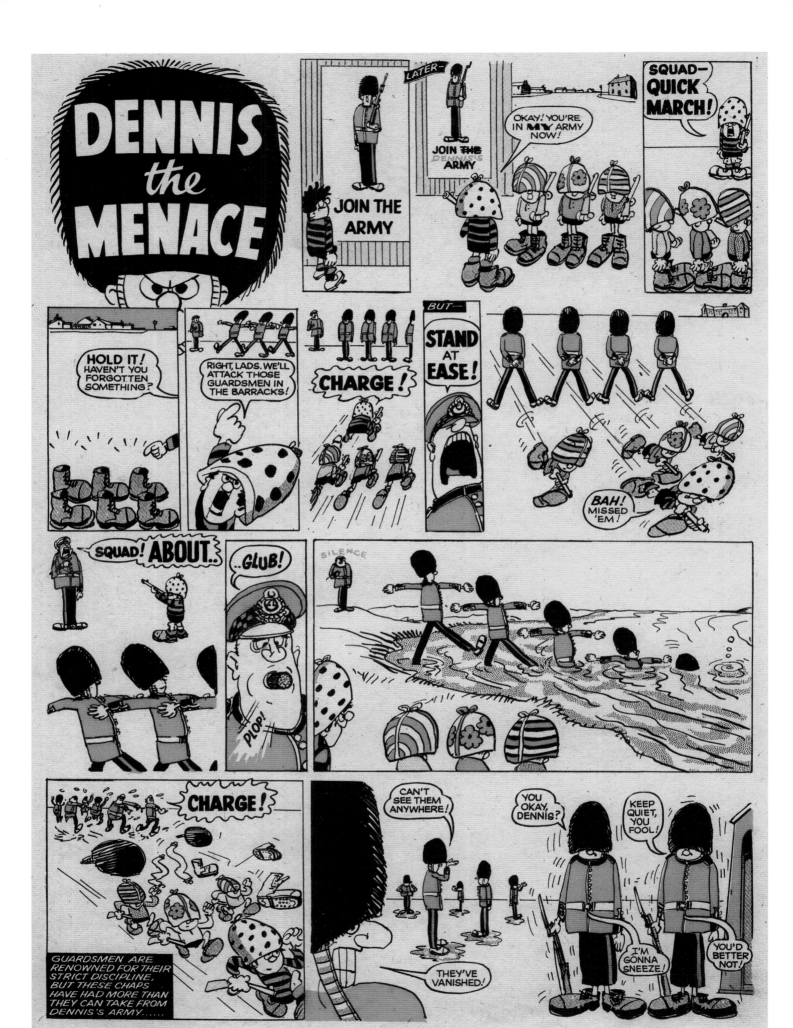

DENNIS THE MENACE

DENNIS the MENACE

DENNIS THE MENACE

OF COURSE WALTER AND WINIFRED WILL WIN THE JUNIOR BALLROOM DANCING CONTEST. YOUR CLUMSY SON WOULDN'T HAVE A HOPE!

SHAME

WE'LL SEE ABOUT THAT!

GRIM

COUSIN DENISE IS STILL STAYING WITH THE FAMILY — I'VE ENTERED YOU IN A CONTEST AGAINST WALTER.

GOOD!

I HOPE IT'S A BOXING CONTEST!

NO! IT'S A BALLROOM DANCING CONTEST!

OH, NO!

LATER — YOU LOOK VERY NICE.

I FEEL A PROPER SOFTIE!

THE CONTEST BEGINS —

TA-RUM-PUM! PUM!

I LOVE DOING THE "MILITARY-TWO-STEP"!

GRACEFUL

DISGRACEFUL

EEK!

I LIKE THE HIGH-KICKING PART!

THUD!

NEXT, "THE QUICK STEP" —

OOPS! THERE GOES MY COLLECTION OF PET BEETLES!

WHIRL

SHRIEK! WHIMPER!

GOING SO SOON?

AAGH! SAVE ME, DADDY! NASTY BEETLES!

SCREECH!

THEN — AS ALL THE OTHER DANCERS LEFT BEFORE THE CONTEST ENDED, THE WINNERS ARE COUPLE THIRTEEN!

PRIDE SHAME

WALTER'S DAD

I'LL NEVER UNDERSTAND DADS! LAST WEEK WE WERE BAD AND GOT SIX OF THE BEST — THIS WEEK WE GOT HALF A CROWN!

DENNIS THE MENACE

Dennis the Menace and GNASHER

A Deadly Duo. Dennis teams up with his doggy pal Gnasher in 1968.

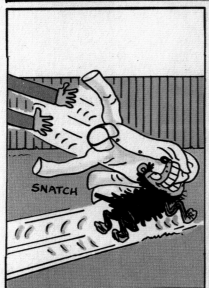

FUNNIER THAN A HIPPO WITH HICCUPS

THE DANDY

55p

Canada $2.50

Dandy Website www.dandy.com email dandy@dcthomson.co.uk Every Saturday No. 3121 September 15th, 2001

THE SMASHER

BULLY BEEF AND CHIPS

...ARE YOU?

LOOK WHAT EVERY MEMBER GETS—

Beano" Reader,
...now a member
...n Club, and here's
...mbership card to
...! Fill in the details
...the card safely in the
...wallet,
...er-always wear your
...es.
    All the best,
        Dennis.

...NT-GNASH-YOWL-SNUFFLE!
...Gnasher saying "Welcome to
...Fang Club, too!")
...Club secrets overleaf!

...nis the Menace Fan Club."

STICK
PHOTO
YOURSELF
HERE.

TOP SECRET

..."Never Good!"
...y Gnasher!"

...S
...y by Fang Club Members.

...SHTY!   Dinner's
           horrible.

...y big sister's always
...ping on at me.

...TTY-   I'm well-
           behaved.

...well-
...ed.

...NIGHT-   Sleep
            well.

CLUB BADGES

There are many ways to wear your badges. Each position has a different meaning.

I read the "Beano" every week.

I need my dinner.

I'm top of my class.

I'm foot of my class.

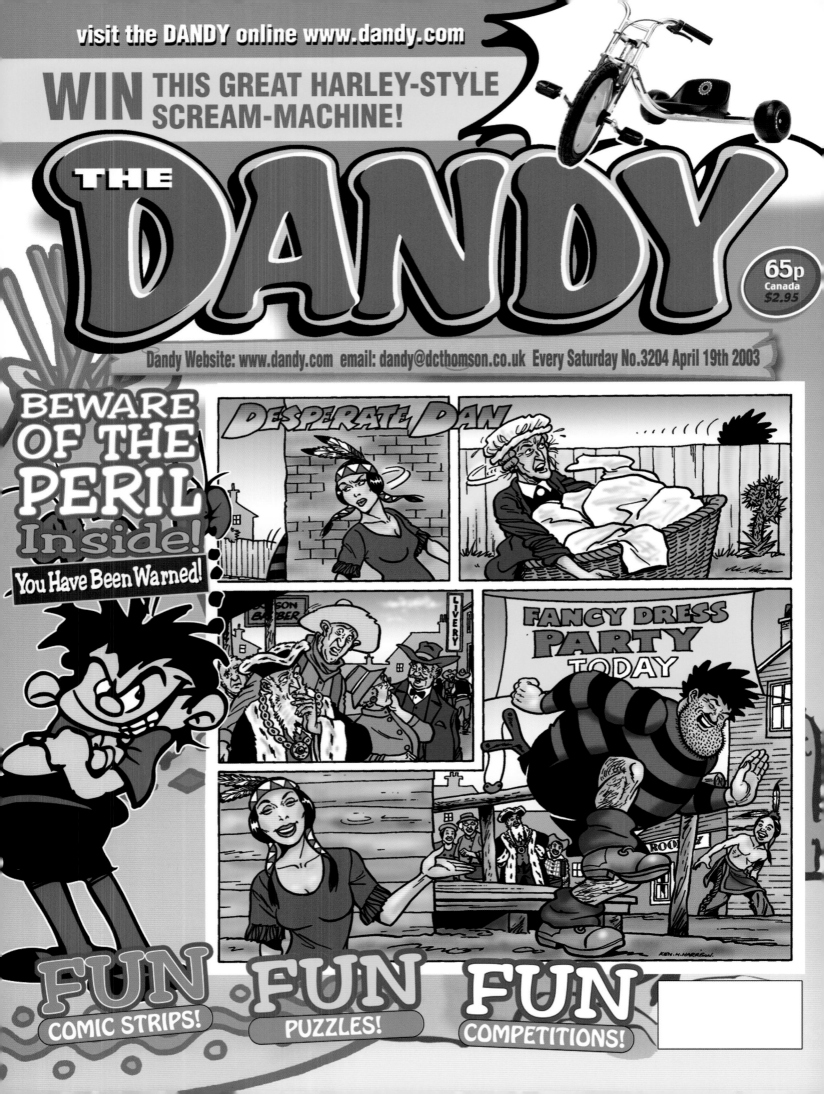

A Birthday Story.

Pin the Tail on the Donkey

Before beginning play, the equipm[ent]
must be set up (see Fig. 2):

Fig.2 : Pin the Tail on the Donkey

NOW, EVERYONE NEEDS TO FIND A PARTNER FOR THIS GAME...

I BAGSY BILLY WHIZZ AS MY PARTNER!

...AND I WANT TO GO FIRST 'COS I'M THE BIRTHDAY BOY!

ALL RIGHT, DENNIS! JUST LET ME EXPLAIN THE RULES!

CHUFFED!

HERE IS A PICTURE OF A DONKEY WITHOUT A TAIL.

NOW, BILLY WILL TRY TO PIN THE TAIL ONTO THE DONKEY'S ...AH....BACKSIDE, WHILST HE'S BLIND-FOLDED...

...AND HIS PARTNER WILL HELP BY SHOUTING DIRECTIONS...!

OKAY, BOYS...?

...READY...

...STEADY...

GO!

BILLY, GO LEFT... ...LEFT A BIT... ...LEFT AGAIN.!

WHOOSH!

THAT'S IT!...KEEP GOING LEFT!

OKAY, NOW GO STRAIGHT ON!

DENNIS IS PRETTY USELESS AT GIVING DIRECTIONS, ISN'T HE?

YEAH ... I MEAN, BILLY IS HEADED...

Pass the Parcel

This popular party game requires a fair amount of preparation.

AAAH!... HAVE YOU GOT A SORE BOTTY, DENNIS..?

PFFF..!

I'LL GIVE YOU A SORE HEAD IF YOU DON'T...

ER... **COULD** YOU ALL PAY ATTENTION, PLEASE ?!

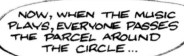

ALL RIGHT, EVERYONE, PLEASE SIT 'ROUND IN A CIRCLE...

NOW, WHEN THE MUSIC PLAYS, EVERYONE PASSES THE PARCEL AROUND THE CIRCLE...

... BUT WHEN THE MUSIC STOPS, THE PERSON WITH THE PARCEL MUST TRY TO OPEN IT AS FAST AS THEY CAN !

THE PLAYER WHO GETS TO UNWRAP THE PRIZE WINS IT !

ER... JUST STICKING IT BACK ON...!

RIGHT ! LET'S START THE GAME !

CLICK!

JACK AND JILL WENT UP THE HILL TO FETCH A PAIL OF WATER...

THIS REALLY IS A BIT SOPPY, DENNIS !

YES, I KNOW...

JACK CAME... *CLICK!*

HEY, IT'S ME !

... THAT'S WHY I'VE BOOBY-TRAPPED THE PARCELS !

RiiiP!

SPLAT!

FLOUR

13

...AND SO, LIKE ALL GOOD THINGS, THE BIRTHDAY PARTY COMES TO AN END...

BYE DENNIS!

SEE YOU IN NEXT WEEK'S "BEANO"!

OOH, LES! DON'T YOU FEEL LIKE SAYING "OINK" ANY MORE?!

SLAM!

WOW! WHAT A GREAT PARTY!

DO WE 'AVE TO CLEAN UP ALL 'DIS MESS?

ARE YOU JOKING? THAT'S WHAT PARENTS ARE FOR!

BUT MUMMY AND DADDY IS NOT HERE!

Dear Dennis,
I've taken your mother away for a couple of days to calm her nerves.
Please take care of Bea and have the house cleaned up for our return.
love,
Dad x

HUH?

THEY CAN'T DO THIS TO ME!

CRACKLE! CRACKLE!

THEY CAN'T EXPECT ME TO CLEAN UP MY OWN MESS!!!

THIS IS OUT-RAGEOUS!

THIS IS A SCANDAL!

D'YOU THINK WE SHOULD TELL DENNIS THAT WE ARE STILL HERE?

NAH... LET'S LEAVE IT A COUPLE MORE MINUTES!

PSSH!

... I THINK WE'RE EARNED OURSELVES A BIT OF PEACE AND QUIET!

I'LL DRINK TO THAT!

CHEERS..!

THE END

DANDY DAYS in BEANOTOWN

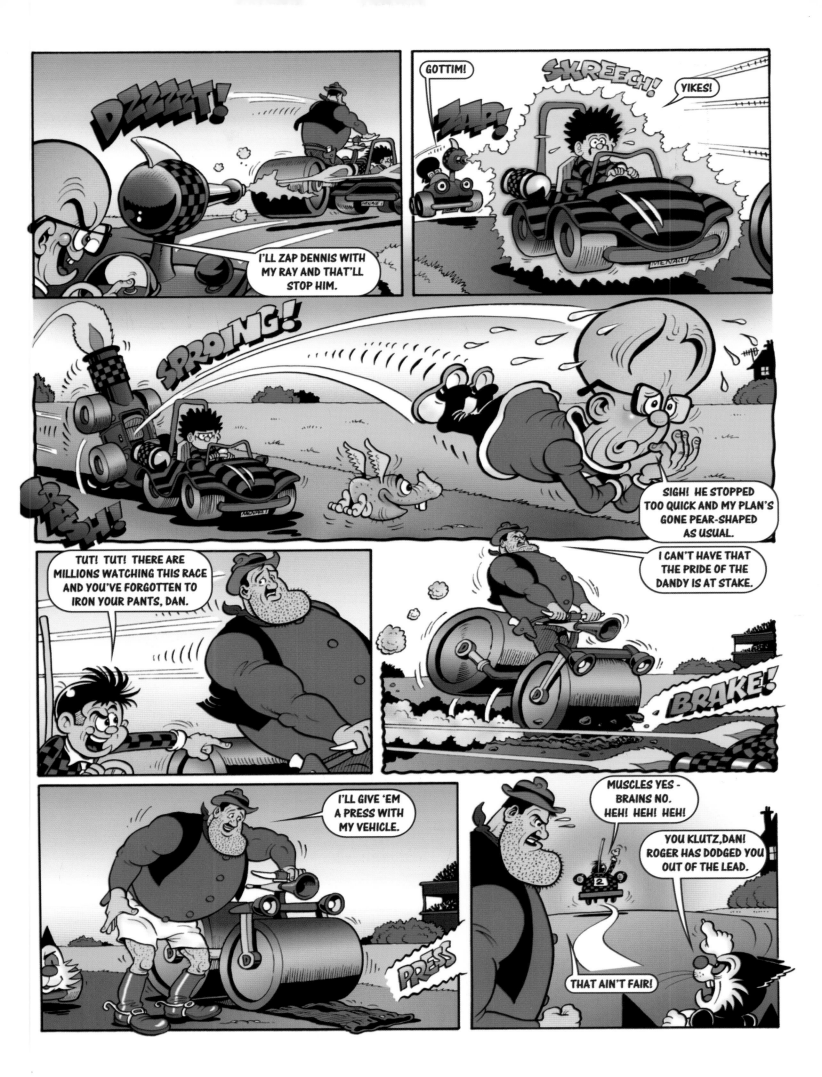

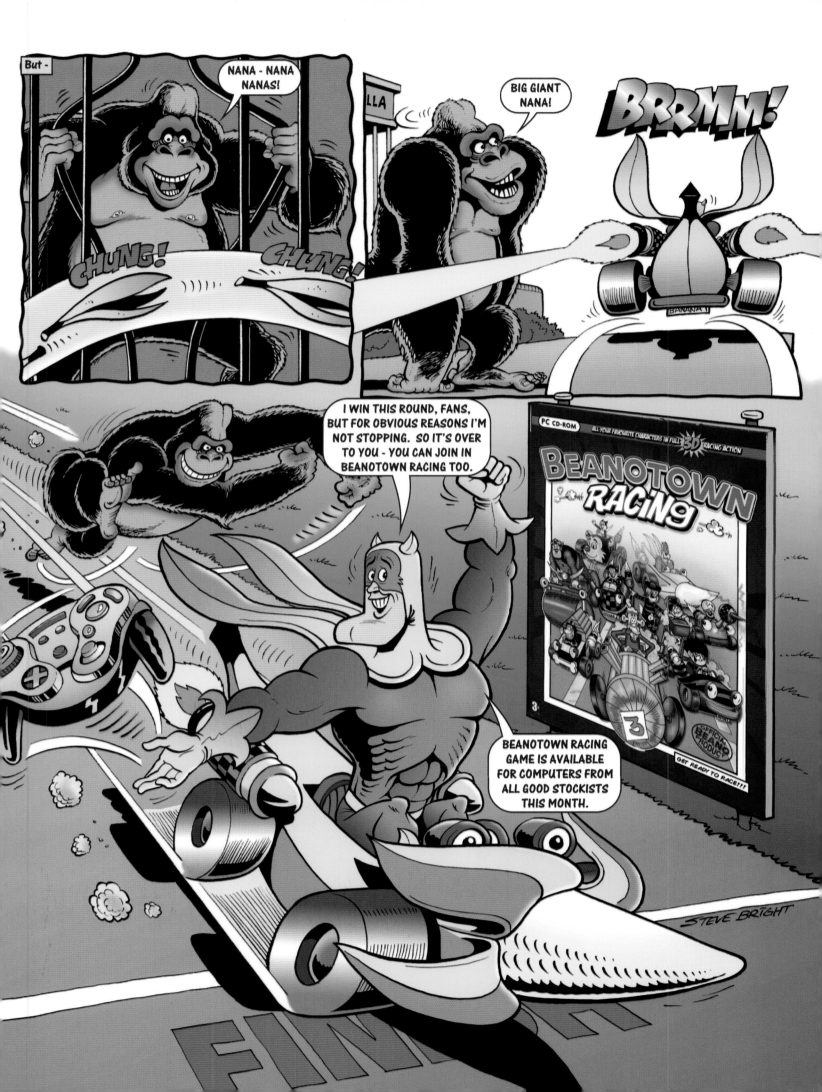

Meet Dennis's new sister in a BIGGER, BRIGHTER

WITH 8 GREAT EXTRA PAGES

THE BEANO

No. 2931 September 19th, 1998   Every Thursday   50p

IT'S A GIRL!

WIN a Legoland Holiday
Join the fantastic new Beano Club INSIDE

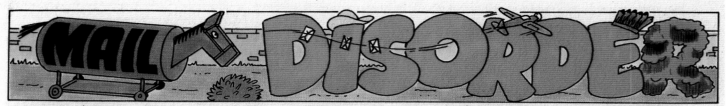

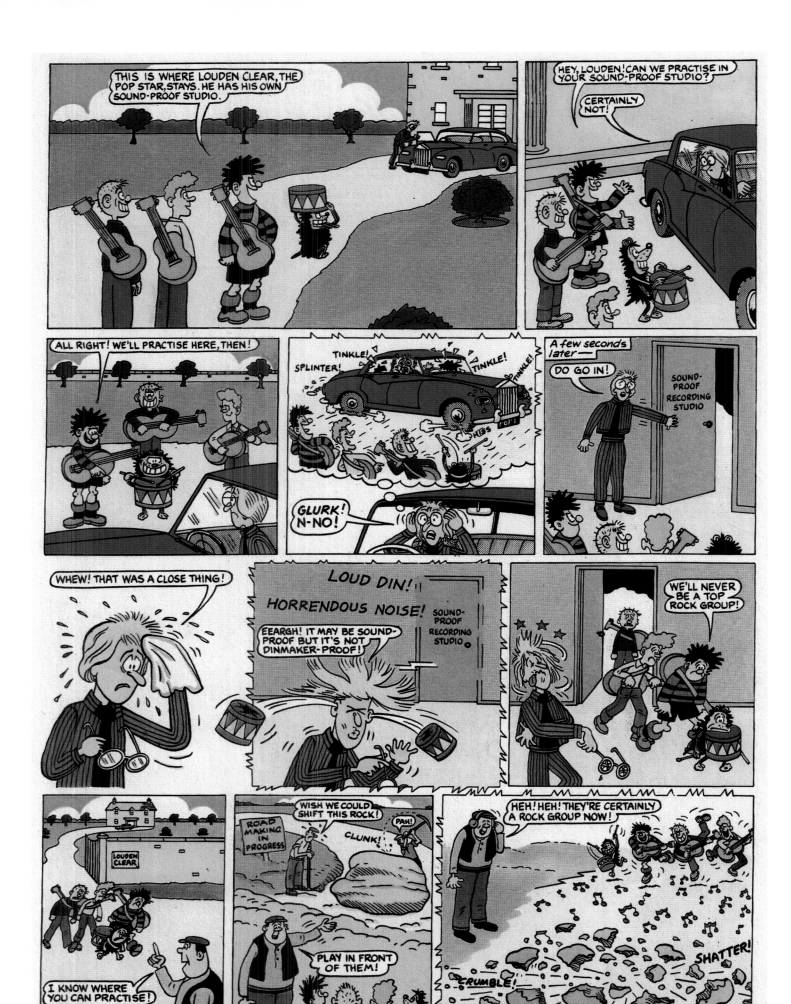

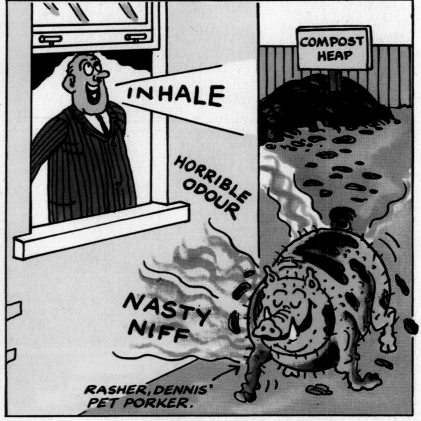

Ok if I bring back a few friends?

For one week only, to celebrate **65** years of the UK's Number One Comic, Dennis has dusted off the cobwebs from some of the original team of stars from July 30th, 1938. Prepare for some fun as today's cast bring the "oldies" right up to date.

< Ping The Elastic Man
The only elastic man in the whole world. Ping often ended up tied in knots.

< Big Eggo
The original cover star, Eggo liked plenty of iron in his diet - kettles, old bikes, coal scuttles - the lot!

Tom Thumb
Only six inches high but he had **BIG** adventures.

< Morgyn the Mighty
A cross between Desperate Dan and Tarzan, Morgyn was cast away on a remote island for many years.

Lord Snooty
Lord Marmaduke of Bunkerton looked a real posh twerp, but he was a normal fun-loving kid at heart.

<Whoopee Hank
Crazy Wild West lawman who, funnily enough, usually got his man.

Uncle Windbag
Elderly relative of a young lad named Billy. Told tales so tall that they disappeared into the clouds.

Tin Can Tommy
Professor Lee and his wife wanted a son, so the Prof made them one out of old pieces of metal.

Hooky's Magig Bowler Hat
After an act of kindness to an Indian carpet seller, Little Hooky Higs was given a magic bowler hat containing a wish granting genie. This sort of thing happened every day back in 1938!

Big Fat Joe
Plump youth who enjoyed himself too much to go to Weight Watchers.

Hairy Dan
Old man - hairy face!

Cracker Jack >
The Wonder Whip-Man who could do all sorts of amazing tricks with a long strand of leather.

DENNIS the MENACE and GNASHER

THE BEANO
BOOK 2001

DENNIS THE MENACE IN ROBOT RUMBLE!

Back in Beanotown —

Dennis and GNASHER

In 2009 a brand new Dennis and Gnasher animated TV series was launched.

Some fabulous design work was done for the series and we were introduced to some great new characters, including-

MRS CREECHER - Dennis's teacher, she's more than aware of the sort of scams Dennis gets up to and she's more than willing to hit him with detention. Which she does regularly.

MR SCRIMP - Dennis's Dad's boss. He's rude, greedy, bad-mannered and bad-tempered. He likes to shout at people, mainly Dennis's dad who he calls 'Whasssisname'.

ATHENA - She is in the same school class as Dennis but her dad is the rock mega star, Ratbucket, and her mum is a supermodel so Athena sees herself as an A-list celebrity. Dennis loves to prank this spoiled, rich girl and her pampered doggy, Miss Mini-Wuff.

Dennis's House and Tree-House.
The Tree-house is where Dennis and his gang go to hang out and play music, games and hatch their plots. It's their special place where all their most secret stuff is kept. There is a sideways lift between Dennis's bedroom and the Tree-house.

Inside the Tree-house.

www.beanotown.com

www.beanotown.com